Holding On While Letting Go

Dr. Sandra Stubbs

Published by Dr Sandra Stubbs, LPC, 2024.

HOLDING ON WHILE LETTING GO

First edition. February 17, 2024.

Copyright © 2024 Dr. Sandra Stubbs.

ISBN: 979-8224853847

Written by Dr. Sandra Stubbs.

To my cherished family, whose unflinching love and supp
the beacon that has led me throughout my life. I would l.
my gratitude to my dearest friends for their constant p
company, and fun. My sincere gratitude goes out to my ha
coworkers, who motivate me to strive for greatness each an
In addition, I would want to express my gratitude to the mei
church community for their unwavering faith, unfailing kin
uplifting spirit. This book is dedicated to each and every on
who have contributed to the enrichment, illumination, and si
of my path. Please accept my gratitude for being a part of n

holding on while letting go
Learning to Heal from Emotional Hurt and Bitterness
FEBRUARY 23, 2024
DRSANDRASTUBBS.ORG
Portland, Oregon

Table of Contents

HOLDING ON WHILE LETTING GO

By Sandra Stubbs, LPC, PhD

3

Introduction

HEALING FROM EMOTIONAL hurt and bitterness is a transforming path that enables individuals to regain their inner peace, happiness, and general well-being. The difficulties we face in life frequently leave us scarred, causing us to bear the burden of old wounds and resentments that limit our capacity to experience joy and love to their fullest extent. However, it is crucial to acknowledge not just the possibility of healing but also the requirement for it to achieve personal progress and to lead a life that is satisfying. In this book, we will delve into the complex process of healing emotional wounds and letting go of bitterness. We will also provide you with insights, techniques, and support to help you get started on this empowering path towards emotional liberation.

The experience will enable you to let go of the past, cultivate self-compassion, and open your heart to a brighter, more satisfying future. Whether you have suffered sorrow, betrayal, or any other type of emotional anguish, this journey will empower you to let go of the past. Let us go together on this transforming path of healing as we find the strength that is within each of us to triumph over the emotional hurt and resentment that we have carried with us.

Holding on and letting go is a tricky balance. However, as humans, we learn to cope and compartmentalize huge and small traumas, transitions, and obstacles in an unhealthy way. In addition, we address historical issues and ideologies that have a negative influence on our relationships. Complications, rejections, and disappointments have become the norm; it's no surprise that so many people are fatigued from sunrise to sunset, never stopping to rest.

Our emotional turmoil is cleverly masked and goes untreated by real professionals. For example, exactly like a worn tire that has driven too many miles, the tread has ragged edges; the automobile routinely loses grip; we detect shakiness or vibration as the car accelerates; and all symptoms of wear and tear are ignored—or missed by eyes that do not want to see them. It is not until one is behind the wheel and hears a loud pop, coming from the exterior of the vehicle that the automobile swerves out of control and, with remarkable elegance, avoids colliding with the car in front of it or maybe an innocent bystander.

No doubt, my friends, life can be cruel to all people equally. "The world breaks everyone afterward; many are strong in the broken places." Ernest Hemingway. While traveling the uncertain road of life, we must notice when the tread is all gone, and life's slippery roads have caused the journey to be unsafe and discouraging. At some point, we must choose to notice as my mom would say, as we hurried from the car to a Sunday morning church service "Girl, come here your slip is hanging". Without warning she would reach her cold hands into the inner sanctum of my skirt and snatch my slip up quickly and say "Y'all, hurry up".

Holding on and letting go entails a range of problematic emotions that must be intentionally manage in order to get the best outcome. Think about a manicured garden; if one delays or avoids the daily tiling of the ground, no matter how hard it may be, weeds will grow.

The fruit that is expected will never mature. Our mental health and psychological well-being are similar to that garden. The mismanaged garden of our mind will only create skewed cognitions, minimize emotional responses, and increase avoidant behaviors.

Therefore, ponder where we have learned to live with mismanaged emotions and thoughts. As children, when we were hurt, when we were learning to walk and fell, we felt the sharp thrust of falling, causing tears to fall out of our eyes. Instinctively, we began to search desperately for someone to soothe the pain. As we age, we learn to say "ouch" as adolescents or teenagers. If it hurts, many of us were bold enough to say so. Consequently, as adults, somewhere between here and there, we have learned to stuff it, push it down, and stash it away selectively, ignoring the pain. Well, at least in the public eye, we found a way to smile and wave.

Nevertheless, in private, we melt into a pool of tears, rejections, and regrets. It is incredible how people can play the Hollywood Academy Award-winning roles in front of others but, behind closed doors, secretly want to die on the inside. The days of waiting on someone to come and rescue us are over. My friends, tag you are the one. There is no better moment than the present to be completely honest with yourself and to fight for those fundamental requirements, which include true love and connection, safety, security, variety, and generosity.

The method of stuffing one's emotions is fraught with a great deal of unintended consequences. To begin, "stuffing it" is nothing more than a training program that trains the brain to accumulate offenses, store resentments, and internalize grudges, all of which might later emerge in nameless disorders of the body. Winch (2014) In the past, we have been subjected to social rejection, isolation, and derision, all of which have contributed to an increased risk of physical violence.

This is because social rejection, isolation, and public humiliation have grown more violent than gang connections, poverty, or drug use. This is owing to the fact that stigma has become more prevalent. These happenings are probably not surprising to you because some of your closest friends have gone through something like or even worse during the past four years. I am confident that this is not anything that surprises you.

I am astounded by it, I concur! Microaggressions, being ignored in a board room at a firm, or being excluded from a meeting with friends are all examples of rejection, discrimination, and isolation. The fact that they failed to invite you to the party is a shocking and convenient oversight on their behalf. We have acquired the ability to tolerate and endure more than is required to bear as a result of the numerous horrifying internal battles that we have experienced. Rejection from one's parents, being abandoned to fend for oneself as a child, or being neglected by members of one's family or by parental figures as a regular routine are all examples of this. The devastation of having partners in firms pretend that you are not present or valuable, and then subtly pushing you aside as a result of this belief. Furthermore, the devastation that engulfs us when a significant other completely forgets special birthdates and relationship anniversaries, the list goes on and on and on. Rejection can be found in many places and most of the time, we are not designed to shoulder this weight.

Could I proceed here? Rejection continues by being bullied by trolls online, are being made to believe that your postings are inconsequential, and it like you are being slighted on social media. Nobody is fond of your post. For the sake of validation and importance, we have developed a habit of counting the number of likes, hearts, and thumbs up subscribers, as if this were a meaningful indicator of the number of people who genuinely care about you. Where does it come to an end? Think about that, is a really interesting question. And.... I go on. Interpersonal hurdles with relationship, arguments, divorce, infidelity, being left out of out of the parental will. What do you do when the family avoids your text messages, phone calls that go ignored and unanswered.

To add insult to injury you finally find a safe place like a church, Bible study group, a community club, and everyone acts like you are invisible. Have you been there? Do you know what I'm talking about? Worse yet, someone approaches your table at a function and speak to everyone at the table, but doesn't look at you.

Rejection may be found anywhere. Because of the level of rejection that people face, these feelings and emotions permeate normal life transitions, such as a young adult leaving for college, which should be a joyous occasion for empty nesters to be together once more in the home that they've built, but instead appears to be betrayal from a parental standpoint. This is a good illustration of absolute dysfunction, as a young adult is shown exiting this hellhole that was once home.

As a General Psychologist, I have witnessed many nuances of devastation from the weak and feeble to the strong and noble, life happens to us all. The house is empty, kids are grown, everyone has their lives, and the senior feels like a burden to the family. The heartbreak of loneliness manifests in the physical discouragement that is felt day by day as they wait for someone to visit. (Rosenbaum, 2007, June 2008)

Holding on while letting go is a notion that encompasses the idea of keeping a sense of connection or attachment to something or someone but simultaneously giving yourself the space and freedom to release and move on. It's a fine balance between clinging on and letting go. The process can apply to various aspects of life, including relationships, emotions and personal growth.

In relationships, hanging on and letting go entails cherishing the link and memories you share with the other person but also acknowledging when your physical presence in this circumstance is costing you more than you are ready to pay. We must realize when it is time to let go and move on. Essentially, I can love and appreciate you better with a distance.

As I pondered this topic of holding on while letting go, I came to realize that the holding on process involves acknowledging the value of the relationship and the lessons learned? While accepting that sometimes people and circumstances change, (for better or worse) and it is necessary to release the attachment in order to find new paths and experiences. It is appropriate to say everything changes the Greek philosopher Heraclitus wrote, 'No man ever steps in the same river twice, for it is not the same river and he's not the same man".

Holding on while letting go entails acknowledging and processing one's emotions and experiences, as well as enabling oneself to heal and evolve. It entails acknowledging the emotions and experiences that have shaped us, as well as recognizing when it is time to let go of any negative or restrictive ideas that may be holding us back. Recognizing the past while simultaneously welcoming the present and the future is the key to achieving a balance in this situation.

When we hold on while letting go, we acknowledge and appreciate the progress and accomplishments we've achieved, while at the same time being open to new opportunities and growth. This is the problem with the closed hand, which is that nothing comes out and nothing comes in. According to a quote attributed to Indira Gandhi, "You cannot shake hands with a closed foot." It is up to us to make the decision to let go, to open up, and to welcome what is ahead. It is necessary for us to maintain the knowledge and abilities that we have gained over this process, while at the same time being willing to let go of outdated habits, beliefs, and behaviors that are no longer beneficial to us. One must have the bravery to venture outside of one's comfort zones and be open to change and transformation in order to achieve this.

Being self-aware, practicing mindfulness, and being willing to accept both the past and the future are all necessary components of the process of holding on while letting go. Finding the right balance between attachment and detachment is a process that may lead to personal development, healing, and a deeper feeling of freedom and fulfillment. It is a process that can lead to these outcomes.

Why is the topic significant for me as a writer? Holding on While Letting Go is how you win and my friends, you will win if you don't quit.

Here are a few things we must hold on to:

1. Maintaining a sense of connection or attachment to something or someone.

2. Cherish the bond of love memories, specifically, those things that add value.

3. Relationships and lessons learn, expecting that people change and grow for the better.

4. Acknowledge your feelings and experiences. Allow yourself to heal and grow.

5. Honoring the encounters and the experiences that has shaped your understanding and has cultivated your growth.

6. New possibilities and expansive ideas, dare to be different.

7. Living in the present moment, that past is just that "past" stay present.

8. Hold on to your faith, hope, love, joy and God fearing community

Here are a few things we should let go of:

1. Mental junk, useless fodder and random information that only makes you upset.

2. Other people's drama, OPD. Say, farewell!

3. The shell of a person that walks in defeat and doubt.

4. Comparing yourself to other people.

5. Grudges, offences, blame, shame, guilt, and excuses

6. Condemnation.

7. Constantly complaining

8. Perfectionism. Life is messy. Learn to thrive despite the mess.

9. Unhealthy habits whether emotionally, physically, psychologically, mentally, or spiritually. Let them go.

10. Worrying about things that are outside of your ability to control.

11. Broken promises and breaking promises.

12. Trying to make everybody happy.

Chapter 1

Healing From Emotional Hurt

DO YOU HAVE EMOTIONAL scars that restrict you from evolving as a human being and as a spiritual person? If so, you need to heal them. Are your emotions consistent with how you live your life? It may be accurate to assume that these problematic emotions are compatible with our daily lives. On the other hand, however, it may be proper to claim that it is difficult to identify whether the feelings of depression, pessimism, or separate experiences are in tune with repeated cycles of hurt and agony in our lives. The vast majority of experts in many academic fields are of the opinion that our individual identities are entirely composed of the sum total of our life experiences.

Emotional wounds have a way of sneaking their way into our lives, and most of the time, we are completely oblivious to the enormous influence that they have. They can make themselves known to us as lingering melancholy, unresolved rage, or a profound sense of acrimony, all of which color our relationships and experiences. If we do nothing to heal these wounds, they might stifle our personal development, keeping us from realizing our full potential and limiting us from enjoying genuine happiness. Because of this, it is of the highest significance to be aware of the signs that these emotional wounds are preventing us from moving on. This awareness will allow us to start the healing process and go on a path of expansion and maturation. In this part of the workbook, we will discuss the telltale indications that show when emotional scars are preventing your progress. This will enable you to take the essential measures toward healing and reclaiming your life.

The research that has been conducted on the topics of emotional wounds and bitterness has thrown light on the enormous influence that these topics may have on our mental, emotional, and even physical well-being.

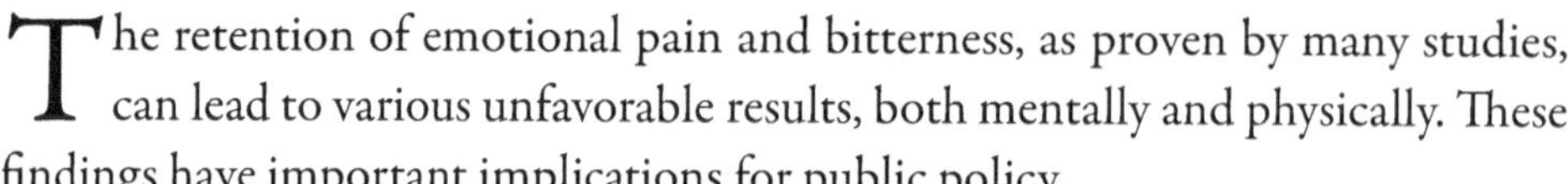

The retention of emotional pain and bitterness, as proven by many studies, can lead to various unfavorable results, both mentally and physically. These findings have important implications for public policy.

Research has been carried out in a variety of fields, one of which focuses on the connection between traumatic experiences and one's mental health. People who harbor anger and emotional suffering that has not been appropriately handled are, according to a number of studies, at a greater risk of developing symptoms of depression, anxiety, and even post-traumatic stress disorder (PTSD). These unpleasant emotions have the capacity to control our thinking, lessen our ability to persevere in the face of hardship, and impede our overall psychological well-being. Research has revealed that emotional scars can have a severe influence on our physical health, which is a major worry. This connection between emotional and physical wounds is a complex one.

Chronic bitterness and emotional pain that has not been addressed have been related to an increased risk of cardiovascular disease, a poorer immune system, increased negative preoccupation, suicidal ideation and even accelerated aging. This is especially true if the emotional suffering has been unresolved.

It is important to note that emotional pain can be felt physically in the body. It is vital to keep in mind that just because there is a link between two things does not mean that one causes the other: in this case, emotional suffering, bitterness, and suicide ideation. Bitterness and resentment can be the result of suffering emotional anguish, such as that caused by a traumatic event, the death of a loved one, or persistent stress. These negative feelings can make an individual's existing emotional suffering much worse and make it more difficult for them to deal with the difficulties of everyday life.

It is possible to experience suicidal ideation, also known as thoughts of terminating one's life, if one is feeling overpowered by emotional agony and believes that there is no hope or any other way to find respite from that pain.

Nevertheless, it is of the utmost importance to approach this subject with care and to acknowledge that the experiences and circumstances of each person are distinct. Suicide ideation does not occur in everyone who goes through emotional pain or bitterness, and not everyone who goes through emotional pain or bitterness has bitterness as a contributing element in their suicide thoughts.

If you or someone you love is having difficulty with any of these concerns, it is imperative to seek the assistance and support of licensed trained professionals.

The stress and negative emotions associated with holding onto bitterness can take a toll on our bodies, leading to various health issues. Fortunately, research has also shown the transformative power of healing emotional wounds and releasing bitterness. Studies have found that engaging in forgiveness practices, seeking therapy or counseling, and cultivating self-compassion can significantly improve mental and physical well-being. Letting go of bitterness and healing emotional wounds has been linked to reduced symptoms of depression and anxiety, improved immune system functioning, and enhanced overall life satisfaction.

In conclusion, research based on data demonstrates the negative consequences of emotional scars and bitterness on our mental, emotional, and physical health. Nonetheless, it also emphasizes the possibility of recuperation and metamorphosis. We may prepare the path for personal development, increased well-being, and a more rewarding existence by addressing and letting go of these emotional scars and, therefore, releasing their hold on us.

Chapter 2

Identifying Emotional Wounds and Bitterness

How can I identify my emotional wounds? The process of determining emotional scars may be quite personal and introspective for the individual doing it.

The following are some essential stages that can assist you in recognizing and naming your emotional scars:

1. Contemplate the lessons learned from the past: Spend some time thinking about key experiences or relationships in your past that may have been emotionally painful. Think back on instances of betrayal, loss, or rejection — or even traumatic experiences — that have left an indelible mark on your feelings.

For each of these experiences consider what did learn from this experience? How do these experiences inform how you manage your relationships? Are these thoughts, images, or behaviors helpful with moving forward to my personal or spiritual goals?

Ques: What story are you telling yourself about your past experiences, life decisions or trauma(s)?

____

Ques: As a result of that experience how do you gain safety? In essence, what behaviors do you to keep yourself safe?

____

Ques: What are the most common emotional responses once you encounter a triggering experience?

____

Ques: Which emotions do you believe or helpful for your healing process?

____

Ques: What would you like to believe about yourself?

____

Ques: How would you respond to challenges if you truly believed that about yourself?

____

2. Pay attention to patterns that keep occurring: Take note if you realize that you have a reoccurring tendency of feeling similar unpleasant emotions or participating in activities that are self-destructive. These patterns might be an indication of unresolved emotional wounds that are impacting the way you think, feel, and behave.

What are the emotional patterns that keep you stuck in internal pain and rejection? Emotional pattern examples: irritated, negative self-talk, sadness, feeling rejected, depression, stuck in negativity shutting down emotionally etc.

____

Ques. What are your negative Emotional patterns:

____

Ques. What do you believe to be true about that experience?

____

Ques. Challenge this thought and think about what else could this mean?

____

Ques. What would you like to believe about yourself?

____

3. Observe your emotional responses: Pay attention to how you respond emotionally to different events or triggers and write down your findings. Do you find yourself experiencing overwhelming feelings of rage, despair, fear, or resentment? These intense emotional responses may be signs of underlying emotional scars that need to be healed.

Are your responses relevantly balanced to what you are experiencing in that present moment? Has there been responses that were disproportionate to the encounter (an overexaggerated response)

Ques. What are your triggers?

Ques. What is within your power to control? How can you work on that part?

---

4. Evaluate your social connections and the way you engage with other people. Evaluate your intimate relationships and the way you engage with people close to you. Do you find it difficult to trust others, to be close to others, or to be vulnerable? Are you quick to judge negatively without having any validated details?

Are you someone who is continually on the lookout or defensive? It's possible that these challenges are the result of emotional wounds that have hindered your capacity to create healthy connections with others.

Practice these responses towards others:

I see (The observation)

Example: I see your frustration.

I need? (Introspection)

Example: I need some time to think this through.

Would you be willing to? (The ask)

Example: Would you be willing to talk about this in a hour over dinner?

Try it for yourself:

I see. (What is your observation?)

I need? (Introspection)

Would you be willing to?

---

5. Pay attention to what your physical body is telling you. Emotional wounds can often leave physical scars. Take note if you suffer from persistent discomfort, tension, or any other physical symptoms that might be related to emotional scars that have not been healed.

Find a comfortable place to sit with your feet on the floor, and for 3 to 5 minutes, just pay attention to your body. Are there aches, pains, strain, fast-moving thoughts, or tightness in the face? Right now, all you are doing is noticing. Your brain automatically tries to figure out why these things are happening. Could it be that you're ignoring your body's normal signs that something is upsetting you? As you sit, take deep breaths into your belly and let your breath move through your whole body.

Identify and write down what you are noticing? There is no good, bad, right or wrong with this exercise. What you notice is what you notice. Allow it be there and when you are ready move on.

Today, I choose to let go (Make your list of items below)

____

I realize that I can hold on to these valuable memories. (Write what makes you laugh, smile, relax, confident, embrace, and love). Choose to keep those things.

____

6. Look for professional assistance: If you feel that it is difficult for you to recognize your own emotional scars on your own, you might think about looking for the assistance of a therapist or counselor. They may be able to provide you with a secure and comforting environment in which you may investigate your feelings, discover the scars that lie beyond the surface, and find your way to healing.

Are you looking for a therapist in your state? Considering reviewing the Psychology Today listing by your state, insurance company, and appropriate costs. As a Christian believer consider a Licensed Professional Christian Counselor or Licensed coach.

Keep in mind that the process of recognizing emotional scars is quite personal, and it may require some time as well as introspection on your part. As you make your way through this process of self-discovery and healing, exercise patience and kindness toward yourself.

Chapter 3

What is Keeping Your Bound to Bitterness

The term "the progression of bitterness" refers to the gradual onset of or increase in the intensity of bitter thoughts, feelings, or behaviors through time. Typically, it comprises a progression of phases or steps culminating in increased bitterness.

The following is a summary of the evolution of bitterness in general:

1. **Initial Disappointment:** The first step to resentment is frequently the experience of disappointment or dissatisfaction. Unfulfilled expectations, the feeling that one has been wronged, or personal failures can all give rise to these feelings.

What is your earliest memory of disappointment, resentment, and/or rejection? When you think of these thoughts what are the perceptions you have concerning yourself? How do you react physically when you are disappointed?

Ques. What are your earliest memories of these triggers? Choose one and explore deeper:

Ques. When you are triggered what are thoughts, feeling, and behaviors?
Thoughts Feelings Behaviors

Ques. As a result of those early memories, what are the thoughts you have about yourself?

Ques. You have the power to choose how to think and feel about that story. Change your story you can change your state.

What would you like to think or feel about that situation?

---

2. **Resentment:** A feeling of animosity might develop if the original disappointment is allowed to last for an extended period. Resentment is a sense of wrath or indignation against someone or something viewed as the source of discontent. Resentment can be directed toward either the person or the object.

Do you have historical anger? How does the anger towards others make you feel about yourself?

Some individuals are passive in their responses to others anger. Therefore, are you a people pleaser? How does that act of pleasing others when they are upset make you feel about yourself?

---

3. **Rumination:** Bitterness tends to be fueled by rumination, which involves dwelling on negative thoughts and replaying past events or perceived wrongdoings. This rumination can intensify the bitterness and make it more challenging to release negative emotions.

Do you have ruminating thoughts? Make a brief list of the negative thoughts and choose a reframe for each?

Example: Rumination: Everyone hates me!

Example. Reframe:

1.) Maybe they do, maybe they don't I haven't met all the people in the world, so I really don't know.

2.) What other people think of me is none of my business.

Try it for yourself.

What are the negative stories ruminating on?

Reframe: Consider using a radical dismissal of the negative thought by using maybe, possibly, I don't know for sure and that's ok.

3. **Blame and Victimhood:** A common characteristic of bitterness is the tendency to place blame on other people or external situations. The individual experiencing bitterness may develop a victim mentality, in which they believe that they have been mistreated or that they have been the victim of a wrong.

Make a list of those people, places, or things that you may blame for what you are experiencing?

I blame (make a list)

Ques. How can you take responsibility for your part ie., your thoughts, feelings, and actions?

4. Isolation and Withdrawal: The experience of bitterness might result in an avoidance of social engagement and the development of new connections. The individual can withdraw inside oneself, avoiding circumstances or people who can trigger flashbacks of their resentment.

Do you tend to op-out of social gatherings, inter-personal settings, groups of people, community activities due to feeling judged and criticized by others? Have these concerns been validated with evidence-based encounters, not your imaginative slights?

Ques. Identify what you are avoiding and label why that causes fear and anxiety?

---

6. **Intensification of Negative Emotions:** Bitterness, when allowed to build up over time, may amplify unpleasant emotions such as wrath, resentment, and jealousy. These feelings can take over a person's life, wreaking havoc on their relationships and other facets of their existence.

When you are sad, angry, frustrated how will others know by looking at your behaviors or facial features?

Consider these questions?

- What am I sad, anger, frustrated, irate about?

- What can I do about this situation, that is not harmful to myself or anyone else?

- What is within my ability to control?

- How can I choose to move forward from this?

Ques. What would you like to change about your behaviors?

7. **Health Consequences:** A lengthy period of bitterness can have negative repercussions on one's physical and mental health, including an increase in stress levels, anxiety, and melancholy, as well as medical difficulties. These negative effects can be caused by an accumulation of bitterness over time.

What are the 5 top stressors you are currently experiencing? In what areas do you perceive underlined bitterness as the fuel for the emotions?

5 Top Stressors:

_1.____2._________________

8. **Difficulty in Letting Go:** It is possible for resentment to become deeply ingrained, making it difficult for a person to let go of unfavorable feelings and move on with their lives.

This can keep a cycle of bitterness going and hinder personal development and healing from taking place.

Reframing Exercise: Make a brief list of 5 items that you may need to "let go" of to move forward? What people, places, or things are holding you back from flourishing?

(Why five items? The number five represents several things such as of Gods goodness and grace, individuality, freedom, the sense of adventure, balance and much more). It is no mystery that we need, grace to be self-applied as we discard old baggage and renew our sense of wellbeing)

Why is grace important? Well we can write and entire chapter on God's grace toward us, in simplistic understanding grace is undeserved kindness bestowed upon us by God, even when we have done nothing to earn it. God has given it to us as a gift at no cost. God's grace have overshadowed your entire life. With fresh eyes, where can you identify God's grace on your life?

Ques. What are five areas people, place, or things that you feel are holding you back from experiencing the fullness of God's grace on your life?

Think about how these things are causing your to be bitter and not better. It is essential to keep in mind that not everyone goes through the stages of bitterness in the same order, and that evolution might differ from one individual to the next. Additionally, reaching out for assistance from loved ones, including friends and family, as well as specialists in the mental health field, can be helpful in addressing and overcoming bitterness.

Chapter 4

Healing the Hurt Through Forgiveness

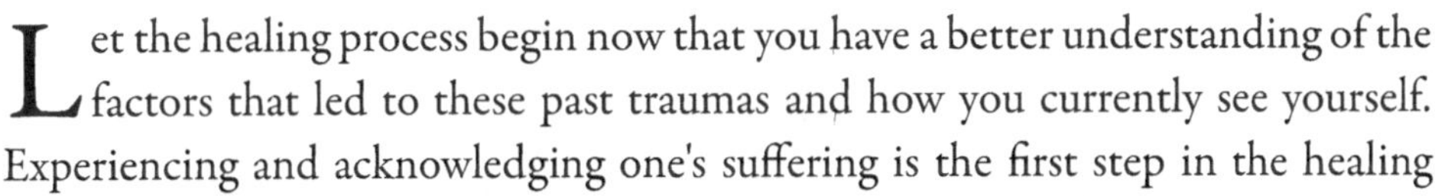

Let the healing process begin now that you have a better understanding of the factors that led to these past traumas and how you currently see yourself. Experiencing and acknowledging one's suffering is the first step in the healing process. Let's take a moment to practice forgiveness.

Although the path to forgiveness and healing is uniquely your own, here are some suggestions that may be helpful:

1. **First, recognize and accept your suffering as real.** Recognize and allow yourself to feel whatever it is you're feeling. Let yourself feel sad, angry, or betrayed if you need to. By repeatedly practicing the acts of forgiving and forgetting, you may teach your brain to let go of the past. Call your emotions into this current reality as often as the trigger warns you, with the aid of your conscious mind and the Spirit of God, who restores all things to our memory. These feelings were once for your highest good (to keep you safe) but are no longer beneficial; thus, we must change.

If you keep thinking about the past and lingering on the past, you may end up providing strength to the bad ideas and unwittingly boosting those sentiments that are holding you back. If you keep thinking about the past and concentrating on the past, you may wind up giving strength to the negative thoughts and dwelling on the past.

Today, I recognize my sufferings are real and are preventing me from living my best life.

Today I commit to the following:

2. Consider the effects of bitterness on your health and happiness and make a daily intentional effort to let go. Realize that forgiveness isn't about ignoring or dismissing the wrongdoing, but about releasing the toxic feelings that have been plaguing you.

I release myself from the following burdens:
ex. Guilt and shame of wrongdoings etc.

Ques. Take five items from your Chapter 3 list of things that are holding you back and practice a reframe. How can these items before a steppingstone to better emotional health?

—— ❧ ——

Ques. How can you take responsibility for your thoughts, feelings, and actions?

3. **Try to perceive things from a new vantage point.** Think about the other person's position, their reasons for responding the way they did, and the potential that they were reacting to your actions because of their own hurt or misunderstanding.

Please note that we are not naive; we know that some people intentionally hurt others by giving in to their evil inclinations, demonic curses, and established beliefs. Consider your intention and ask God to disclose the enemy's evil agenda. Then, you will unmask your true power and discover that the enemy desires to eliminate you and, thus, your impact on the world. When you're ready to view things differently, you will see that you are truly unstoppable.

4. **Develop compassion and empathy by imagining what it would be like to be in the other person's position.** This doesn't mean you should condone their actions, but you should recognize that they, like you, are human and so prone to error.

I accept myself. I accept my flaws and imperfections. How can you use acceptance to move away from difficult emotions?

5. **Establish limits:** Forgiveness does not obligate you to get back together with or maintain contact with the person who wronged you. Setting up safe limits is crucial for preventing additional injury.

What are implementable boundaries you can set for your life?

---

6. **Find healthy outlets for your negative emotions, such as wrath, resentment, and bitterness.** Doing things like talking to a close friend or therapist, writing in a diary, working out, or meditating can all help.

Choose your confidants wisely. Who in your circle of influence will love you, pray for you, tell you the truth, and continue to be your friend even if you two don't agree?

---

7. **Take care of yourself by participating in activities that improve your physical, emotional, and mental health the highest priority in your self-care routine.** This might involve indulging in hobbies, getting adequate sleep, maintaining a good diet, exercising regularly, and seeking support from friends and family.

My daily routine of self-care/God's care. Write the plan. How will I take care of my physical body as well as keeping my spiritual house clean?

---

8. **Consider enlisting the assistance of a licensed therapist or counselor who will be able to walk you through the stages of the forgiving process.** They are able to provide you with a secure environment in which you may investigate your feelings and counsel that is suited to your unique circumstance. Keep in mind that forgiving others is a personal journey that might take some time.

Have patience with yourself while you recover and give yourself permission to get better at your own rate.

Chapter 5

Healing Through Self - Compassion

HOW CAN WE DEVELOP compassion for oneself and others? Since we live in a culture that places a lot of emphasis on accomplishment, productivity, and other forms of external validation, we frequently fail to show the same level of compassion and understanding toward ourselves as we do toward others. We tend to get stuck in a vicious loop of self-criticism, self-judgment, and self-doubt, which can impede our capacity to heal and progress as individuals.

But imagine for a moment if we were able to break out of this pattern. What if we were able to heal our wounds and nourish our souls by drawing upon the transformational power of self-compassion?

Through the cultivation of self-compassion, we will traverse a path leading to the discovery of oneself, the acceptance of oneself, and the healing of oneself during this journey.

Decide to learn more about the amazing benefits of self-compassion, self-understanding, and self-acceptance for your health and wellbeing. Self-compassion has a transformative quality that causes a positive mental transformation. In the end, this change establishes a cognitive alignment pathway. For instance, the relationship between the mind, body, and soul is shown by thinking about and acting with more self-compassion toward yourself. The first step on the road to liberation is the mind. You can escape the psychological prison if you can think your way out of it.

We will acquire the skills necessary to notice our own suffering, give credence to our feelings, and develop a profound sense of self-kindness. We can liberate ourselves from the shackles of self-judgment and self-criticism when we practice self-compassion. This opens the door for us to heal and mature in ways that we never believed were possible.

This workbook will help you incorporate self-compassion into your day-to-day life by providing you with useful tools, exercises, and insights. The wisdom of ancient philosophies, psychology research, and personal tales were all drawn from in the creation of this book. You will learn how to cultivate mindfulness, how to confront your own self-judgment, and how to connect with the shared humanity that unites all of us.

You may learn to negotiate the obstacles that life throws at you with grace and resilience if you engage in self-care practices, such as setting healthy boundaries and seeking assistance when you feel you need it.

"Healing Through Compassion" is more than simply a statement; it's a guide to discovering oneself and finding one's own path to recovery. It is an invitation to set out on a journey of self-actualization, during which you will learn the depths of your own resilience, capacity for love, and strength. You will not only be able to heal your own wounds if you practice self-compassion, but you will also set off a chain reaction of compassion and empathy that will spread to everyone around you.

To that end, would you say that you are prepared to go on this road of self-improvement? Are you prepared to make self-compassion the compass that you use to navigate your life? In that case, let's get started. Together, we are going to take one compassionate step at a time as we make our way along the road to healing, self-discovery, and loving ourselves.

Self-healing via self-compassion means treating yourself with kindness, understanding, and acceptance, particularly when circumstances are challenging. Putting self-compassion into practice involves the following steps:

1. **Recognize your suffering:** Recognize the anguish you are experiencing; acknowledge and affirm the pain, problems, and feelings you are going through. Realize that pain is an inevitable part of the human experience, and that it is perfectly normal for you to feel the way that you do.

Suffering can exist in many domains' family, career, health, finances, emotional baggage etc. Here are a few questions to start the thinking process.

Ques. **What area do you experience the most suffering?**

Ques. How has this suffering progressed over the years?

Ques. What is the story you tell yourself about your suffering?

---

2. **Practice self-kindness:** You should show yourself the same amount of compassion and attention that you would give to a loved one. Always remember to treat yourself with kindness and compassion, especially when you screw up or are confronted with a hardship.

If you met someone that was going through a similar situation as you, what advice would you give them? How would you show them comfort and support? How would you apply that advice to yourself?

---

3. **Practice mindfulness by being more aware of your internal experiences—including your thoughts, feelings, and bodily sensations—without passing judgment on them.** The practice of mindfulness enables one to notice their experiences without engaging in self-criticism or other forms of destructive internal dialogue.

How can I practice mindfulness in the absence of people?

- Pray and meditate on a scripture of encouragement or strength.
- Listen to calming soothing sounds or music.
- Having a healthy meal or snack reset the digestive system.
- Take a walk.
- Snuggle a pet.
- Take a nap, rest your worry mind.

What are other ways you may practice mindfulness?

---

4. **Observe and question the ideas and beliefs that you have about yourself that are judgmental and critical.** Change your internal monologue to one that is kinder and more grounded in reality. Remind yourself that no one is flawless and that making errors and having flaws is an inevitable aspect of being human.

Who Am I? What are adjectives that describe who you are becoming?
Ex. I am strong. I am courageous. I am gifted.

---

5. **Establish a connection with other people who share your humanity and realize that you are not alone in the challenges you face.** At some time in their lives, everyone will be confronted with challenges and will feel the sting of suffering. Get in touch with other people who may have had similar experiences, and keep in mind that you are not the only person going through this struggle.

Who are my support people? Who can I reach out to for emotional support and/or prayer?

---

6. **Engage in activities that are beneficial to your overall health and well-being as a kind of self-care that you should practice.** This might include things such as obtaining a enough amount of sleep, eating nutritious food, exercising, spending time in nature, pursuing hobbies, or participating in activities that offer you joy and relaxation.

What are motivating activities I can do with others?

---

7. **Learn to say "no" when it's appropriate and create healthy boundaries in the relationships you have by learning how to say "no."** Put your own requirements and well-being first, and don't be afraid to ask for assistance from other people whenever you feel you need it.

When was the last time you declined an invitation that was extended to you? Keep in mind that even if you answer "no" today, you may always answer "yes" tomorrow. Do not withdraw inside oneself as a means of coping with the emotional anguish; instead, fight the feelings, make an effort, and do the challenging tasks.

---

8. **If you are coping with profound emotional scars or trauma, you should consider obtaining support from a therapist or counselor who can lead you**

through the healing process. Consider taking your workbook with you and sharing some of your insight with your professional. If you are unsure whether or not you need professional assistance, read on.

Keep in mind that self-compassion is a discipline that requires both time and effort on your part. Be kind and patient with yourself and make developing self-compassion a lifetime practice that serves as a tool for both healing and personal development.

Thoughts?

____

____

Chapter 6

Seeing A Counselor for the First Time

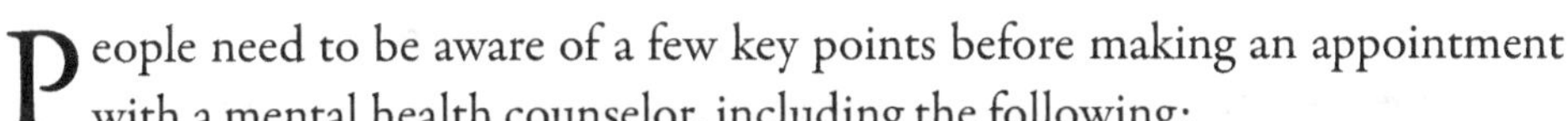

People need to be aware of a few key points before making an appointment with a mental health counselor, including the following:

1. **Confidentiality:** Therapists are required to adhere to stringent confidentiality standards, the material that is said during therapy sessions is often not disclosed to anybody outside of the therapeutic relationship. Having said that, there are a few circumstances in which this rule can be bent, such as when the therapist has reason to suspect that there is a potential for the client or other people to come to harm. Before beginning treatment, it is essential to have a complete comprehension of the confidentiality policy that will be followed by the therapist.

2. **Goals and expectations:** It is beneficial to have a distinct goal in mind for what you anticipate achieving via treatment. Talk to the therapist about your objectives and what you want to achieve throughout treatment to make sure you're both on the same page. This will be helpful in guiding the treatment process and ensuring that you are working towards the objectives that you desire..

3. **Therapeutic approach:** Different therapists may use different therapeutic approaches or techniques. It can be helpful to research and understand the various approaches to therapy, such as cognitive-behavioral therapy (CBT), psychodynamic therapy, or mindfulness-based therapy. This knowledge can help you choose a therapist whose approach aligns with your preferences and needs.

4. **Time commitment:** Therapy is not a quick fix and often requires a significant time commitment. It's important to understand that progress may take time and that therapy is a process. Discuss with your therapist how

frequently you will be meeting and for how long, as well as the estimated duration of therapy.

5. **Financial considerations:** Therapy can be costly, so it's important to understand the financial aspects before starting. Check if your insurance covers therapy and what your out-of-pocket expenses may be. If therapy is not covered, discuss the therapist's fees and payment options to ensure that it is affordable for you.

6. **Openness and honesty:** Therapy is most effective when there is open and honest communication between the client and therapist. It's important to be willing to share your thoughts, feelings, and experiences openly, as this will help the therapist better understand your situation and provide appropriate guidance.

7. **Building rapport:** Building a strong therapeutic relationship is crucial for successful therapy. It may take some time to find the right therapist with whom you feel comfortable and connected. Don't hesitate to try out different therapists until you find the one that feels right for you. Remember, therapy is a collaborative process, and it's important to actively participate and engage in the process to get the most out of it.

Conclusion

When confronted with emotional suffering and resentment, the road to recovery and flourishing may appear to be an insurmountable obstacle. Nevertheless, if we equip ourselves with the power of authenticity and self-compassion, we have the ability to triumph over our challenges and embrace a life that is filled with resilience, development, and joy. Throughout the entirety of this workbook, we have investigated the transforming power of self-compassion as a driving force behind the healing process.

We have developed the ability to acknowledge our own pain, give credence to our feelings, and relate to ourselves with compassion and comprehension. We discovered that we are not alone in our struggles because we challenged our own self-judgment and connected with our shared humanity. However, recovery is not the final objective; rather, it is only the first step. We must not only learn to survive challenging times, but we must also learn to flourish. To truly thrive, we must acknowledge the value of the insights gained through our suffering and apply those insights as building blocks on the path to our own development and satisfaction. Being resilient, adaptable, and having the desire to embrace change are all necessary traits for thriving in challenging circumstances. It entails developing an attitude of appreciation and discovering delight in the mundane activities that make up daily life.

It includes putting healthy boundaries in place, making self-care a top priority, and reaching out for assistance when you feel you need it. It involves making the most of our talents and interests and working toward living a life that is congruent with our principles and goals. As we engage on this path toward prospering, it is imperative that we recognize that we will inevitably face obstacles and roadblocks along the way.

However, if we have compassion for ourselves, we will be able to confront these challenges with poise and resiliency. We can grow from our errors, to forgive ourselves for those mistakes, and to keep going ahead with the same level of tenacity and confidence that got us here.

Keep in mind that recovering from wounds and prospering are not always sequential processes. These are not destination points; rather, they are never-ending, ever-changing journeys that call for patience, self-reflection, and self-compassion. Through the use of these techniques, we have the ability to change our suffering into wisdom, our resentment into empathy, and our challenges into sources of strength.

I want to therefore urge you to carry the teachings of emotional healing, forgiveness, self-compassion and thriving with you. Embrace the transformative power of self-compassion as a guiding light in your life and allow it to illuminate the route that leads to your own recovery and development.

Take on the difficulties that lie in wait for you, confident in the knowledge that they are opportunities for growth and for demonstrating your resiliency. Most importantly, show yourself love, compassion, and understanding. You should give yourself permission to accept all the healing and growth that this world has to offer because you are deserving of it.

Your path, however difficult it may be, needs to be accompanied with self-compassion, fortitude, and the unwavering belief that you have the capacity to develop and heal even in the most trying situations.

Addendum
Believers Bonus I

Those who are suffering might find solace, hope, and encouragement in the words of the Bible, which include counsel and wisdom on the subject of mending emotional scars. The following is a list of some of the ways in which the Bible portrays the process of emotionally mending wounds:

1. **Seek God's comfort:** are grieving and that he offers solace to those who require it. According to Psalm 34:18, "The Lord is close to the brokenhearted and saves those who are crushed in spirit." The Lord is near to the brokenhearted, as this passage says. By praying to God and seeking his presence, we might find solace and healing for our emotional scars. By doing this, we shall get closer to God.

2. **Receive God's love and forgiveness:** The love and forgiveness of God are shown as important themes throughout the Bible. God declares in

Isaiah 43:25, "I, even I, am he who blots out your transgressions, for my own sake, and remembers your sins no more." This refers to God's willingness to forgive people's wrongdoings. The release of feelings of guilt, shame, and self-condemnation, which can lead to emotional healing, can occur when we get an understanding of, and acceptance of,

the love and forgiveness of God.

3. **Practice forgiveness:** The Bible imparts the wisdom that it is necessary to forgive others in order to find personal restoration. It is said in the book of Ephesians Chapter 4 verse 32, "Be kind and compassionate to one another, forgiving each other, just as in Christ God forgave you." The ability to forgive makes it possible for us to let go of resentment and bitterness, which releases us from the emotional load and makes it possible for us to recover.

4. **Renew your mind:** The Bible exhorts us to refresh our minds and center our attention on things that are edifying and beneficial. Romans 12:2 states, "Do not conform to the pattern of this world, but be transformed by the renewing of your mind." This is a reference to the pattern of this world. We can experience healing and transformation in our lives if we choose to replace toxic thinking patterns and negative self-talk with the truth and promises found in God's word.

5. **Seek wise counsel and community:** The significance of seeking the assistance and sound advice of others is emphasized repeatedly throughout the Bible. According to Proverbs 11:14, "Where there is no guidance, a people falls," but "where there is an abundance of counselors, there is safety." On the road to emotional recovery, it can be helpful to cultivate good connections, seek advice from respected elders or counselors, and become active in communities that offer emotional support in order to get solace, encouragement, and direction.

6. **Trust in God's plan:** Even when we are in the middle of suffering, the Bible encourages us to put our faith in the plan and purpose of God. It is said in the book of Proverbs 3:5-6, "Trust in the Lord with all your heart, and do not lean on your own understanding; in all your ways submit to him, and he will make your paths straight." Hope and healing for our emotional scars may be found when we believe that God is sovereign and that He can create beauty from our brokenness. This belief can bring us to place our trust in God.

While these biblical principles can serve as a guide, it is essential to keep in mind that the process of healing emotional scars is a multifaceted and uniquely personal endeavor.

On the path to emotional recovery, it can be helpful to seek the advice and aid of trustworthy spiritual leaders, counselors, or therapists. Doing so can give further direction and assistance.

Healing Scriptures II

The Bible is filled with various texts that provide solace, support, and direction for the purpose of emotional development and healing. As you progress through each chapter of the program, you might want to think about how meditating on scripture might help you reframe the conversation that you have with yourself.

Scripture by Chapter Reference:

Chapter 1: Healing from Emotional Hurt

MATTHEW 6:34; "THEREFORE do not be anxious about tomorrow, for tomorrow will be anxious for itself. Sufficient for the day is its own trouble."

Matthew 6:27; "And which of you by being anxious can add a single hour to his span of life?"

James 1:2-4; "Count it all joy, my brothers, when you meet trials of various kinds, for you know that the testing of your faith produces steadfastness.

Joshua 1:9; "Have I not commanded you? Be strong and courageous. Do not be frightened, and do not be dismayed, for the Lord your God is with you wherever you go".

Philippians 4:6-7; "Do not be anxious about anything, but in everything by prayer and supplication with thanksgiving let your requests be made known to God. And the peace of God, which surpasses all understanding, will guard your hearts and your minds in Christ Jesus."

Psalm 6:2; "Have mercy on me, Lord, for I am faint. Heal me, Lord, for my bones are in agony."

Philippians 4:19; "And my God will meet all your needs according to the riches of his glory in Christ Jesus.

Chapter 2: Healing from Bitterness

PSALM 147:3 - "HE HEALS the brokenhearted and binds up their wounds."

Isaiah 41:10 - "So do not fear, for I am with you; do not be dismayed, for I am your God. I will strengthen you and help you; I will uphold you with my righteous right hand."

Matthew 11:28-30 - "Come to me, all you who are weary and burdened, and I will give you rest. Take my yoke upon you and learn from me, for I am gentle and humble in heart, and you will find rest for your souls. For my yoke is easy and my burden is light."

2 Corinthians 1:3-4 - "Praise be to the God and Father of our Lord Jesus Christ, the Father of compassion and the God of all comfort, who comforts us in all our troubles, so that we can comfort those in any trouble with the comfort we ourselves receive from God."

Proverbs 16:24; "Gracious words are a honeycomb, sweet to the soul and healing to the bones."

Psalm 34:17-18 - "The righteous cry out, and the Lord hears them; he delivers them from all their troubles. The Lord is close to the brokenhearted and saves those who are crushed in spirit."

Philippians 4:6-7 - "Do not be anxious about anything, but in every situation, by prayer and petition, with thanksgiving, present your requests to God. And the peace of God, which transcends all understanding, will guard your hearts and your minds in Christ Jesus."

1 Peter 5:7 - "Cast all your anxiety on him because he cares for you."

Psalm 30:2 - "Lord my God, I called to you for help, and you healed me."

Jeremiah 17:14 - "Heal me, Lord, and I will be healed; save me and I will be saved, for you are the one I praise." 10. Psalm 42:11 - "Why, my soul, are you downcast? Why so disturbed within me? Put your hope in God, for I will yet praise him, my Savior and my God."

Scriptures like this serve as a constant reminder of God's love, consolation, and power to heal. They inspire us to turn to Him in times of emotional sorrow, worry, and trouble, knowing that He is near and ready to heal and restore our hearts and minds. They also remind us that He is with us.

John 14:27; "Peace I leave with you; my peace I give you. I do not give to you as the world gives. Do not let your hearts be troubled and do not be afraid."

Malachi 4:2; "But for you who fear My name, the sun of righteousness shall rise with healing in its wings. You shall go out leaping like calves from the stall."

Notes:

Chapter 3: What's Keeping You Bound to Bitterness

JAMES 5:16; "THEREFORE confess your sins to each other and pray for each other so that you may be healed. The prayer of a righteous person is powerful and effective."

Isaiah 33:2; "Lord, be gracious to us; we long for you. Be our strength every morning, our salvation in time of distress."

Proverbs 17:22; "A healing heart is good medicine, but a crushed spirit dries up the bones."

Acts 8:23; For I see that you are full of bitterness and captive to sin."

Colossians 3:8; But now you must also rid yourselves of all such things as these: anger, rage, malice, slander, and filthy language from your lips.

Colossians 3:13 Bear with each other and forgive one another if any of you has a grievance against someone. Forgive as the Lord forgave you.

Ecclesiastes 7:9; Do not be quickly provoked in your spirit, for anger resides in the lap of fools.

Ephesians 4:26; 26 "In your anger do not sin" : Do not let the sun go down while you are still angry,

Ezekiel 3:14; 14 The Spirit then lifted me up and took me away, and I went in bitterness and in the anger of my spirit, with the strong hand of the LORD on me

Job 21:25; Another dies in bitterness of soul, never having enjoyed anything good.

Job 7:11; "Therefore I will not keep silent; I will speak out in the anguish of my spirit; I will complain in the bitterness of my soul".

Notes:

Chapter 4: Healing Through Forgiveness

PSALM 119:50; "THIS is my comfort in my affliction, that your promise gives me life."

Exodus 23:25; "Worship the Lord your God, and his blessing will be on your food and water. I will take away sickness from among you."

John 14:27; "Peace I leave with you; my peace I give you. I do not give to you as the world gives. Do not let your hearts be troubled and do not be afraid."

Ephesians 4:32 - Be kind and compassionate to one another, forgiving each other, just as in Christ God forgave you.

Matthew 6:14 - For if you forgive other people when they sin against you, your heavenly Father will also forgive you.

Mark 11:25 - And when you stand praying, forgive, if you have anything against anyone, so that your Father also who is in heaven may forgive you your trespasses.

Colossians 3:13 - Bearing with one another and, if one has a complaint against another, forgiving each other; as the Lord has forgiven you, so you also must forgive.

Luke 23:34 - And Jesus said, "Father, forgive them, for they know not what they do."

Isaiah 38:17; Surely it was for my benefit that I suffered such anguish. In your love you kept me from the pit of destruction; you have put all my sins behind your back.

Notes:

Chapter 5: Healing Through Self Compassion

PROVERBS 4:20-22; "MY son, give attention to my words; incline your ear to my sayings. Do not let them depart from your eyes; keep them in the midst of your heart; for they are life to those who find them, and health to all their flesh.

Isaiah 41:10; "So do not fear, for I am with you; do not be dismayed, for I am your God. I will strengthen you and help you; I will uphold you with my righteous right hand."

James 5:14; "Is anyone among you sick? Let them call the elders of the church to pray over them and anoint them with oil in the name of the Lord."

Psalms 146:8; "The Lord gives sight to the blind, the Lord lifts up those who are bowed down, the Lord loves the righteous."

Psalm 23:4; "Even though I walk through the darkest valley, I will fear no evil, for you are with me; your rod and your staff, they comfort me."

Psalm 73:26; "My flesh and my heart may fail, but God is the strength of my heart and my portion forever."

Psalm 119:50; "This is my comfort in my affliction, that your promise gives me life."

Notes:

Chapter 6: See a Counselor for the First Time

PROVERBS 13:10 - ONLY by pride cometh contention: but with the well advised is wisdom.

Proverbs 15:22 - Without counsel purposes are disappointed: but in the multitude of counsellors, they are established.

Proverbs 20:5 - Counsel in the heart of man is like deep water; but a man of understanding will draw it out.

What type of therapy do I need? Most common approaches

Trauma Related: PTSD

Anxiety Related: Mindfulness, Acceptance & Commitment Therapy

Mood Dysregulation: Behavioral Activation, Dialectical Behavioral Therapy

Life Transitions: Cognitive Behavioral Therapy, Integrative Approaches, Life Coaching

Obsessive Compulsive Disorders & related illness: Exposure Response Prevention, Acceptance Commitment Therapy, Habit Reversal Training, Cognitive Behavioral Approach

ENDNOTES

SECTION ONE

FILELLA GUIU, G., & Ros Morente, A. (2023). Happy Software: An interactive program based on an emotion management model for assertive conflict resolution.

Gilbert, Pehl, and Allan (1994). The phenomenology of shame and guilt: An empirical investigation. British Journal of Medical Psychology

Lerner, H. G. (2014). The dance of anger: A woman's guide to changing the patterns of intimate relationships. HarperCollins.

Luskin, F., & Pelletier, K. R. (2005). Healing your emotional self: A powerful program to help you raise your self-esteem, quiet your inner critic, and overcome your shame. John Wiley & Sons.

Mackie, D. M., Smith, E. R., & Ray, D. G. (2008). Intergroup emotions and intergroup relations. *Social and Personality Psychology Compass*, 2(5), 1866-1880.

Winch, G. (2014). *Emotional first aid: Healing rejection, guilt, failure, and other everyday hurts*. Penguin.

Smedes, L. B. (1996). Forgive and forget: Healing the hurts we don't deserve. HarperOne.

Zech, E., & Rimé, B. (2005). Is talking about an emotional experience helpful? Effects on emotional recovery and perceived benefits. Clinical Psychology & Psychotherapy: An International Journal of Theory & Practice, 12(4), 270-287.

SECTION TWO

CAMPBELL S. BEING DISMISSED: The Politics of Emotional Expression. *Hypatia.* 1994;9(3):46-65. doi:10.1111/j.1527-2001. 1994.tb00449.x

Flanders, C. (2006). Shame and the Meaning of Punishment. Clev. St. L. Rev., 54, 609.

Gorski, P. C. (2011). Unlearning deficit ideology and the scornful gaze: Thoughts on authenticating the class discourse in education. *Counterpoints, 402,* 152-173.

Kerrigan, W. (1998). Of Scorn. *George Herbert Journal 22*(1), 143-163. https://doi.org/10.1353/ghj.2013.0063.

Kohm, S. A. (2009). Naming, shaming and criminal justice: Mass-mediated humiliation as entertainment and punishment. Crime, Media, Culture, 5(2), 188-205.

Mason, Michelle (2003). Contempt as a moral attitude. Ethics 113 (2):234-272.

Ratcliff, N. J., Franklin Jr, R. G., Nelson, A. J., & Vescio, T. K. (2012). The scorn of status: A bias toward perceiving anger on high-status faces. *Social Cognition, 30*(5), 631-642.

Scappaticci, A. L. S. S. (2011). Bitterness in the search for emotional experience analysis of a child. *Jornal de Psicanálise, 44*(81), 187-202.

SECTION THREE

FLEURY, C. (2022). Here Lies Bitterness: Healing from Resentment. John Wiley & Sons.

Islam, T., Chaudhary, A., & Ali, H. F. (2023). A bitter pill to swallow: the model of despotic leadership, bullying behavior, emotional intelligence and well-being. European Journal of Training and Development.

Mulyani, S., Lumingkewas, M. S., & Hutabarat, C. (2023). The Effect of Restoring Your Heart (RYH) Ministry, Finding Roots of Bitterness, and Emotional Management, on Heart Healing: A Quantitative Study in Indonesia. Pharos Journal of Theology, 104(3).

Scappaticci, A. L. S. S. (2011). Bitterness in the search for emotional experience analysis of a child. *Jornal de Psicanálise*, *44*(81), 187-202.

Stedman, R. (1969). Breaking the Resentment Barrier. Rompimiento de la barrera del resentimiento")(sermón presentado en la Iglesia Bíblica de Península, Palo Alto, California,

Treasures of the Parable Series-Serie Tesoros de las parábolas-, mensaje 11 del 13 de julio de 1969), pág, 6.

Tylim, I. (2005). The power of apologies in transforming resentment into forgiveness. International Journal of Applied Psychoanalytic Studies, 2(3), 260-270.

SECTION FOUR

EHRING, T. (2021). Thinking too much: rumination and psychopathology. *World Psychiatry*, *20*(3), 441.

McCarrick, D., Prestwich, A., Prudenzi, A., & O'Connor, D. B. (2021). Health effects of psychological interventions for worry and rumination: A meta-analysis. *Health Psychology*, *40*(9), 617.

Watkins, E. R., & Roberts, H. (2020). Reflecting on rumination: Consequences, causes, mechanisms and treatment of rumination. Behaviour Research and Therapy, 127, 103573.

Zawadzki, M. J. (2015). Rumination is independently associated with poor psychological health: Comparing emotion regulation strategies. Psychology & Health, 30(10), 1146-1163.

SECTION FIVE

DONALD, J. N., CIARROCHI, J., Parker, P. D., Sahdra, B. K., Marshall, S. L., & Guo, J. (2018). A worthy self is a caring self: Examining the developmental relations between self-esteem and self-compassion in adolescents. Journal of personality, 86(4), 619-630.

Lander, A. (2019). Developing self-compassion as a resource for coping with hardship: exploring the potential of compassion focused therapy. Child and Adolescent Social Work Journal, 36(6), 655-668.

Neff, K. (2003). Self-compassion: An alternative conceptualization of a healthy attitude toward oneself. Self and identity, 2(2), 85-101.

Neff, K. D. (2003). The development and validation of a scale to measure self-compassion. *Self and identity*, 2(3), 223-250.

Neff, K. D., & Dahm, K. A. (2015). Self-compassion: What it is, what it does, and how it relates to mindfulness. *Handbook of mindfulness and self-regulation*, 121-137.

Neff, K., & Knox, M. C. (2016). Self-compassion. *Mindfulness in positive psychology: The science of meditation and wellbeing*, 37, 1-8.

Wasylyshyn, K. M., & Masterpasqua, F. (2018). Developing self-compassion in leadership development coaching: A practice model and case study analysis. International Coaching Psychology Review, 13(1), 21-34.

| Page

Don't miss out!

Visit the website below and you can sign up to receive emails whenever Dr. Sandra Stubbs publishes a new book. There's no charge and no obligation.

https://books2read.com/r/B-A-MTWDB-LIAXC

BOOKS2READ

Connecting independent readers to independent writers.

About the Author

Dr. Sandra Stubbs is a doctor of psychology and licensed professional counselor. For over 20 years she has followed the passion to help hurting people recover through Faith and mental health. Sandra began her work with parents and children as a navigator for the department of human services, teaching parents how to navigate the stress of the DHS system. She saw out professional counseling as a young pastor in effort to understand the perplexities of faith and mental health and to make a difference. Dr. Stubbs has authored two books Finish Strong maintaining the audacity to speak peace in the mist of the storm, and the Finish Strong workbook, which can be found on Amazon, sites. Her podcast Dr. Sandra Stubbs, faith and mental health inspire listeners to recognize the delicate balance that occurs between Faith and mental well-being. She is a champion for integrating Faith mental health and she encourages listeners to notice the delicate balance that exist between the two. As a result of her courageous approach to living a Christian life, she is able to bring about a change that is both long lasting and significant, and the lies and circumstances of other people.finished

Read more at www.drsandrastubbs.org.

About the Publisher

Sandra G. Stubbs, LPC, PhD

    Self Published

    2.24.2024

    sandra.stubbs@ifscenterllc.com

    Copyright @ DrSandraStubbs 2024

    ISBN: 979-8-224-85384-7

Although I am a therapist, I am not your specific therapist. Reading the contents of this manuscripts is not counseling or relationship advice and does not constitute a therapeutic relationship between us. The Workbook must be used as a substitute for the advice of a competent therapist admitted or authorized to work in your jurisdiction.

Read more at https://www.drsandrastubbs.org/.